T0245367

BIG BOYS DON'T CRY

Written by: Victoria Walker

© 2022 Victoria Walker. All rights reserved.

No part of this book may be reproduced, stored in a retrieval system, or transmitted by any means without the written permission of the author.

AuthorHouse™
1663 Liberty Drive
Bloomington, IN 47403
www.authorhouse.com
Phone: 833-262-8899

Because of the dynamic nature of the Internet, any web addresses or links contained in this book may have changed since publication and may no longer be valid. The views expressed in this work are solely those of the author and do not necessarily reflect the views of the publisher, and the publisher hereby disclaims any responsibility for them.

This book is printed on acid-free paper.

ISBN: 978-1-6655-7545-4 (sc)
ISBN: 978-1-6655-7546-1 (hc)
ISBN: 978-1-6655-7544-7 (e)

Library of Congress Control Number: 2022920995

Print information available on the last page.

Published by AuthorHouse   11/29/2022

author HOUSE®

For my brothers. May you never stop nurturing the little boys within the remarkable men that you are.

Cam and PawPaw woke up early one Saturday morning to go fishing. "We've gotta get going, Fellowman. I like to get to the fish before the sun does," the grandfather said as he placed a plate of breakfast in front of Cam.

Cam loved PawPaw's breakfast. His grandfather's biscuits and eggs were his favorite. The biscuits were always baked perfectly golden, and the eggs were fluffy with a hint of cheese. But what he loved most about his grandfather's breakfast was the talks the two had while eating.

"PawPaw, can I ask you a question?" Cam looked up at his grandfather. "Yesterday, you told me that big boys don't cry. Why is that, Pop? Why don't big boys cry? I'll be a man soon, so I need to know."

The old man shook his head and smiled.

"Because big boys are tough," he said, "especially when they grow to become men."

4

The grandfather's words lingered in the boy's mind as the day went on. While fishing, Cam tried to hook his own bait, but it was just too slimy. His hand slipped, and the hook missed the bait pricking his finger. His eyes watered as he watched his grandfather place the Band-Aid over the small area of skin. Cam did not cry.

Then, Cam tried to walk to the front of the boat, but the water's current made the boat rock from side to side.

He was almost there, until…

FLOOP!

He slipped and fell
face first onto the boat's
slimy, smelly floor.

"YUCK!"
he thought.

11

12

"You ok back there?" PawPaw called from the front of the boat. Cam nodded his head with a quivering lip. Still, he did not cry.

The two continued to fish all morning and throughout the afternoon. By the end of the day, PawPaw had caught eight fish. Cam had only caught one. He hung his head and fiddled with his fingers as the two traveled to shore.

Still, Cam did not cry.

16

The next morning, PawPaw was preparing breakfast again. The smell traveled throughout the house, making its way into Cam's room. "Yes!" he thought as he sprang out of bed.

The two sat and talked about their fishing trip, math class, aliens, and anything else that Cam could think of.

"Oh, darn. We'll be late if we don't get a move on," PawPaw interrupted. Cam finished the last bites of his breakfast and raced to change into his church clothes. He buttoned his shirt to the very top and tucked it into his pants. He fastened his belt, tied his shoes, and grabbed his tie from the bed as he headed for his grandfather's room.

PawPaw knelt on one knee and placed the tie over the boy's head and onto his neck. His hands begin to gently do what they always do – work. "What do you think?" his grandfather asked as the two stood before the mirror examining the tie.

"I think I'm ready for church, PawPaw," the boy smiled. The grandfather's eyes begin to water. He loved the little boy so much. As he stood from his knee, he wiped a tear from his eye.

"PawPaw?" Cam was puzzled. "You told me that big boys don't cry."

24

The grandfather thought carefully this time before responding. "Crying is how people express themselves, Cam. Sometimes it is because they are happy. Other times, it is because they are not so happy, but it is never because they are small, Grandson." Cam looked at his grandfather with tears in his eyes, and this time he did not try to hide them.

Because big boys cry, too.

Printed in the United States
by Baker & Taylor Publisher Services